American Revolution and Those of Government, and Its Armed Forces

Texas 1845.
1846–1847. 28 stars.

Iowa 1846.
1847–1848. 29 stars.

Wisconsin 1848.
1848–1851. 30 stars.

California 1850.
1851–1858. 31 stars.

Minnesota 1858.
1858–1859. 32 stars.

Oregon 1859.
1859–1861. 33 stars.

Kansas 1861.
1861–1863. 34 stars.

West Virginia 1863.
1863–1865. 35 stars.

Nevada 1864.
1865–1867. 36 stars.

Nebraska 1867.
1867–1877. 37 stars.

Colorado 1876.
1877–1890. 38 stars.

North Dakota, South Dakota, Montana, Washington 1889. Idaho 1890.
1890–1891. 43 stars.

Wyoming 1890.
1891–1896. 44 stars.

Utah 1896.
1896–1908. 45 stars.

Oklahoma 1907.
1908–1912. 46 stars.

New Mexico, Arizona 1912.
1912–1959. 48 stars.

Alaska 1959. Hawaii 1959.
1960. 50 stars.

The President of the United States.

Vice President of the United States

Secretary of Defense.

U.S. Army.

U.S. Navy.

U.S. Air Force

Secretary of State.

Secretary of Agriculture.

This book is dedicated to the memory of
David S. Pallister Jr.
Captain, U.S.A.F.
June 22, 1944–June 4, 1969

Text and interior illustrations copyright © 1973 by Peter Spier
Jacket art copyright © 2014 by Peter Spier

All rights reserved. Published in the United States by Doubleday, an imprint of Random House Children's Books,
a division of Random House LLC, a Penguin Random House Company, New York.
Originally published in a different form by Doubleday & Company, Inc., Garden City, New York, in 1973.

Doubleday and the colophon are registered trademarks of Random House LLC.

Visit us on the Web! randomhouse.com/kids

Educators and librarians, for a variety of teaching tools, visit us at RHTeachersLibrarians.com

Library of Congress Cataloging-in-Publication Data is available upon request.
ISBN 978-0-385-37618-1 (trade) — ISBN 978-0-375-97209-6 (lib. bdg.)

MANUFACTURED IN CHINA

10 9 8 7 6 5 4 3 2 1

The STAR-SPANGLED BANNER

PETER SPIER

Doubleday Books for Young Readers

O say can you see by the dawn's early light

What so proudly we hail'd at the twilight's last gleaming,

Whose broad stripes and bright stars

through the perilous fight

O'er the ramparts we watch'd were so gallantly streaming?

And the rockets' red glare, the bombs bursting in air,

Gave proof through the night that our flag was still there.

O say does that star-spangled banner yet wave

O'er the land of the free and the home of the brave?

On the shore dimly seen through the mists of the deep,

Where the foe's haughty host in dread silence reposes,

What is that which the breeze, o'er the towering steep,

As it fitfully blows, half conceals, half discloses?

Now it catches the gleam of the morning's first beam,

In full glory reflected now shines in the stream.

'Tis the star-spangled banner—O long may it wave

O'er the land of the free and the home of the brave!

O thus be it ever when freemen shall stand

Between their lov'd home and the war's desolation!

Blest with vict'ry and peace,

may the heav'n-rescued land

Praise the power that hath made

and preserv'd us a nation!

Then conquer we must,

when our cause it is just,

And this be our motto, "In God is our Trust."

And the star-spangled banner in triumph shall wave

O'er the land of the free and the home of the brave.

Words by
FRANCIS SCOTT KEY
(1779-1843)

Music by
JOHN STAFFORD SMITH
(1750-1836)

Chorus:
a little slower

proof through the night that our flag was still there. O say does that star-span-gled

ban-ner yet wave o'er the land of the free and the home of the brave?

2.

On the shore dimly seen through the mists of the deep,
Where the foe's haughty host in dread silence reposes,
What is that which the breeze, o'er the towering steep,
As it fitfully blows, half conceals, half discloses?
Now it catches the gleam of the morning's first beam,
In full glory reflected now shines in the stream.
'Tis the star-spangled banner—O long may it wave
O'er the land of the free and the home of the brave!

3.

And where is that band who so vauntingly swore
That the havoc of war and the battle's confusion
A home and a country should leave us no more?
Their blood has wash'd out their foul footsteps' pollution.
No refuge could save the hireling and slave
From the terror of flight or the gloom of the grave.
And the star-spangled banner in triumph doth wave
O'er the land of the free and the home of the brave.

4.

O thus be it ever when freemen shall stand
Between their lov'd home and the war's desolation!
Blest with vict'ry and peace, may the heav'n-rescued land
Praise the power that hath made and preserv'd us a nation!
Then conquer we must, when our cause it is just,
And this be our motto, "In God is our Trust."
And the star-spangled banner in triumph shall wave
O'er the land of the free and the home of the brave.

O say can you see ~~through~~ by the dawn's early light,
What so proudly we hail'd at the twilight's last gleaming,
Whose broad stripes & bright stars through the perilous fight
O'er the ramparts we watch'd, were so gallantly streaming?
And the rocket's red glare, the bomb bursting in air,
Gave proof through the night that our flag was still there,
O say does that star-spangled banner yet wave
O'er the land of the free & the home of the brave?

On the shore dimly seen through the mists of the deep,
Where the foe's haughty host in dread silence reposes,
What is that which the breeze, o'er the towering steep,
As it fitfully blows, half conceals, half discloses?
Now it catches the gleam of the morning's first beam,
In full glory reflected now shines in the stream,
'Tis the star-spangled banner — O long may it wave
O'er the land of the free & the home of the brave!

And where is that band who so vauntingly swore,
That the havoc of war & the battle's confusion
A home & a Country should leave us no more?
~~Their blood~~
— Their blood has wash'd out their foul footstep's pollution.
No refuge could save the hireling & slave
From the terror of flight or the gloom of the grave,
And the star-spangled banner in triumph doth wave
O'er the land of the free & the home of the brave.

O thus be it ever when freemen shall stand
Between their lov'd home & the war's desolation!
Blest with vict'ry & peace may the heav'n rescued land
Praise the power that hath made & preserv'd us a nation!
Then conquer we must, when our cause it is just,
And this be our motto — "In God is our trust,"
And the star-spangled banner in triumph shall wave
O'er the land of the free & the home of the brave. —

This is the poem Francis Scott Key wrote in his Baltimore hotel room during the night of September 14, 1814, after witnessing the bombardment of Fort McHenry. The poem originally had no title. Key gave it to his brother-in-law J. H. Nicholson the next day. This copy remained in the Nicholson family for almost a century, but the Maryland Historical Society bought it in 1953 for $26,400.

The Story of
"The Star-Spangled Banner"

The story of our country's national anthem began in a conflict far from American soil. It was 1805, and England and France were engaged in the Napoleonic wars. England needed all its commercial ships and merchant sailors for the war effort, so they were unavailable for importing and exporting goods. To take advantage of this void, America quickly jumped in and began to dominate trade between the West Indies and Europe. The British tried to stop America from sending goods to France by insisting that its ships first touch at an English port for inspection. At the same time, the French banned the import of any cargo into its territory that had been cleared by the British. America was caught in between.

In 1807, President Thomas Jefferson tried to force Britain and France to lift their restrictions on American shipping by closing all American ports to international trade. This, however, turned out to be disastrous: tobacco, wheat, and lumber piled up in warehouses and the hoped-for results were not achieved.

War Declared

The British Navy, in need of ever more men, began boarding American ships to catch British deserters, often taking Americans as well. America's temper, already on edge after years of trade disputes, flared. On June 18, 1812, the United States declared war on Great Britain—a conflict that we now know as the War of 1812. The United States was only thirty-six years old, and yet it was already fighting Great Britain again, in a war for which the young nation was unprepared.

In August 1812, the British invaded and took Detroit, and in October an American attack on the British position at the Niagara River failed. At sea, things went better for the Americans: USS *Constitution* was victorious against HMS *Guerriere*, and USS *United States* captured HMS *Macedonian*. But this period of victory did not last. In 1813, the British Navy captured scores of American ships. The Atlantic coast was blockaded.

Many New England merchants, depending heavily on world trade and opposed to the war from the start, now became openly hostile to American participation in the conflict. But the war continued. The British conducted landings and raids, each time withdrawing to the safety of their ships.

Meanwhile, things had gone well for England and its allies in the Napoleonic wars: the French were defeated in 1813, and Napoléon abdicated in April 1814. England was now free to concentrate her efforts on that bothersome distant war in the New World.

The original receipt for payment for the flag that flew over Fort McHenry shows that Mary Young Pickersgill was paid $405.90 for sewing "1 American Ensign 30 by 42 feet first quality Bunting" and $168.54 for sewing a smaller flag. The original flag is now prominently displayed in the National Museum of American History at the Smithsonian Institution in Washington, DC.

Baltimore Attacked!

On August 19, 1814, a mighty British fleet entered Chesapeake Bay with a professional army of thousands, and on August 24 they defeated the raw American militia at Bladensburg, Maryland. They then captured Washington, DC (at that time a small town of six thousand), and burned the Capitol, the White House, and other government buildings. On August 25, afraid of being cut off from their supplies, the British left the city and returned to their ships.

They now turned their attention to Baltimore, the country's third-largest city, with forty thousand inhabitants. The Americans had expected this and had greatly fortified the city's defenses. To strengthen Fort McHenry, guarding the shore, they sank twenty-four ships' hulls as underwater blockades, placed booms from ships' riggings across the north branch of the Patapsco River, and manned all the outlying fortifications. On September 11, the British fleet arrived at the mouth of the Patapsco River, and Baltimore's church bells called the militia to arms.

The next day, the British landed and began moving toward the city. They had planned to take it from both land and sea, but Fort McHenry, protected by one thousand troops, stood solidly in the way of the ships. Shortly after 12:30 in the morning on September 13, the British attempted to land a thousand men at Ferry Branch to attack the fort from the rear, but they were discovered and retreated downriver. Meanwhile, British ships were bombarding the fort, an attack that lasted for twenty-five hours. On the morning of September 14, they withdrew. The assault had failed.

Between 1,500 and 1,800 shells had been fired at the fort, and it seems a miracle that only four American troops were killed and twenty-four wounded. On land, the British did not fare much better. Facing the firmly entrenched Americans on the city's outskirts, the British decided that taking Baltimore without naval support would prove too costly, so they retreated. They re-embarked the next day and sailed toward the open Atlantic.

A peace treaty was signed on December 24, 1814. But news traveled slowly in those days, and the last battle of the war was fought more than two weeks later, when Major General Andrew Jackson defeated the British at New Orleans on January 8, 1815. The war had accomplished nothing for either side, but a witness to the bombing of Fort McHenry gave the country something totally unexpected: a national anthem.

An Anthem Conceived in Battle

During their withdrawal from Washington, the British had arrested Dr. William Beanes, a physician from Upper Marlboro, Maryland, who had detained some British soldiers after they were caught stealing. Francis Scott Key, a friend of Dr. Beanes, practiced law in Georgetown. Armed with a letter from President James Madison, he and John Stuart Skinner, a U.S. agent in charge of prisoner exchanges, left Baltimore to find HMS *Tonnant*, where Dr. Beanes was imprisoned. There, the British granted their request for Dr. Beanes's release, persuaded by letters that told of British soldiers' gratitude for medical treatment from Dr. Beanes.

The men were forced to stay on their American boat instead of returning to land, however, as they had

FRANCIS SCOTT KEY, 1779–1843
Portrait by DeWitt Clinton Peters, after an original attributed to Rembrandt Peale.

learned too much about the British plans for attacking Baltimore. So it was there, around dawn on September 13, that they watched the beginning of the bombardment of Fort McHenry.

The attack continued in full force throughout that day and the next night, but in the dawn's early light on September 14, Key saw a flag hanging over the fort. At first, he was unable to tell whether it was British or American. Then the breeze slowly unfolded the stars and stripes. The Americans had won the battle.

Key had been writing poetry for years and, greatly moved, jotted down a stanza on the back of a letter he carried in his pocket. That night in his hotel, he finished the first draft of the poem. He showed it to his brother-in-law, who liked it so much that he had it printed immediately as "Defence of Fort McHenry" in a local newspaper and suggested that a well-known old tune called "To Anacreon in Heaven" would go well with it.

On September 20, several other papers printed the poem, too, and in October the program at a Baltimore theater announced, "After the Play, Mr. Harding will sing a much admired SONG, written by a gentleman of Maryland, in commemoration of the GALLANT DEFENSE OF FORT MCHENRY, called THE STAR-SPANGLED BANNER."

Over the years, it gained so much in popularity that in 1889 the Secretary of the Navy ordered it to be played at all flag raisings. And in 1916, President Woodrow Wilson announced that the song would be played at all military events. But it was not until 1931 that it became the country's national anthem.

A Flag's Journey

The flag that flew over Fort McHenry had an interesting journey from 1814 onward. Lieutenant Colonel George Armistead, who had been the commander of Fort McHenry during the attack, kept the flag at his home as a souvenir. It was passed from generation to generation as a family heirloom, and pieces were occasionally cut off to give away as gifts. The flag had originally measured thirty by forty-two feet, but as pieces were cut off, the length was reduced to thirty-four feet.

As "The Star-Spangled Banner" became popular as a song, interest in the flag grew. A descendant of Armistead loaned it to Baltimore for the city's 150th anniversary in 1880, but then moved it to a vault for fear the flag would deteriorate. In 1912, he donated the flag to the Smithsonian Institution so that it could be shared with the American people.

In 1914, the Smithsonian attempted to preserve the flag by attaching it to a linen backing with over 1.7 million stitches. But as technology advanced, in 1998 the Smithsonian was able to embark on its most complex and modernized restoration yet. Teams of conservators removed all the stitches holding the flag to the backing, then painstakingly cleaned and repaired it in a specially designed lab.

The flag is now preserved on display in a climate-controlled chamber in the Smithsonian's National Museum of American History, so that visitors from around the world may view this national treasure for many years to come.

THE FLAG MOVES TO THE SMITHSONIAN: When it arrived in July 1907, the star-spangled banner was hung on the exterior of the Smithsonian Institution building (the "Castle") to be photographed. The assistant secretary of the Smithsonian wrote to Eben Appleton, who had donated the flag, "The newspaper men are after me, and they all want a photograph of it to publish in the various local papers. . . . Its presence in the Museum has caused a wave of patriotism, which is very good to see."

Secretary of Commerce.

Secretary of the Interior.

Attorney General.

Sec'y. of Labor.

Postmaster General.

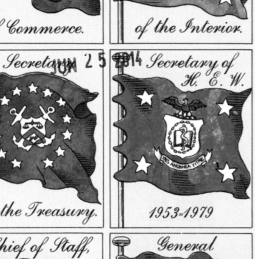

Secretary of the Treasury.

Secretary of H.E.W. 1953-1979

Chief of Staff, U.S. Air Force.

General, U.S. Air Force.

Group Standard, U.S. Air Force.

Chief of Staff, U.S. Army.

General of the Army.

General, U.S. Army.

Major General, Medical Corps.

Major General, Chaplains Corps.

Headquarters, Army Ground Forces.

Marking Pennant, Commission Pennant.

Organizational Color, U.S.A.

Organizational Standard, U.S.A.

Adj. General Maryland National Guard.

Color, U.S. Corps of Cadets.

Survey Flag, Coast and Geodetic Survey.

Director, Coast and Geodetic Survey.

Consular Boat Flag, Foreign Service.

Customs Service. 1789-2003

Yacht Owners Pennant, Naval Reserve.

Yacht Ensign.

Geological Survey.

Director, Fish and Wildlife Service.

Surgeon General, Public Health Service.